Don't Hate the Player, Hate the Game is an incredibly informative and easy reading tool for all age groups. This book *educates* boys and girls, men and women about the objective of the game and how to make informed decisions to avoid getting played! It *encourages* the reader to recognize their priceless self-worth and to feel confident in the standards they set for themselves. Ultimately, this book *empowers* girls and women to commit to their standards and to gain control over the relationships in which they choose to enter. This book is a great reference for young people to keep with them while growing through life experiences.

—**Tonya Marie Lee,**
Women's Track and Field Coach
The University of Georgia

don't hate
the player
hate game
the

don't hate the player hate the game

a girl's guide to benching the bad boys

Robert Williams

TATE PUBLISHING & *Enterprises*

Published by Tate Publishing & Enterprises, LLC
127 E. Trade Center Terrace | Mustang, Oklahoma 73064 USA
1.888.361.9473 | www.tatepublishing.com

Tate Publishing is committed to excellence in the publishing industry. The company reflects the philosophy established by the founders, based on Psalm 68:11,
"The Lord gave the word and great was the company of those who published it."

Book design copyright © 2008 by Tate Publishing, LLC. All rights reserved.
Cover design by Janae J. Glass
Interior design by Leah LeFlore

Published in the United States of America

ISBN: 978-1-60604-148-2
1. Juvenile Nonfiction, Soc. Sit., Dating & Sex   2. Family & Relationships, Adolescent, General/Sexuality
08.08.20

Dedication

I dedicate this book to all the beautiful young girls who will one day be the women that will mother the world.

A special thanks to my loving wife, Denese, for the past twenty-two wonderful years, who has gracefully encouraged me to complete this book, and our two sons, Curtis and Joshua, who will not play the game. To Dr. Victoria Pettis for all her help and encouragement, my friend Harold Waters, and my entire Timothy and Old Storm Branch Baptist Church Families, and to the staff and students of Clarke Middle School, the best middle school in the world. Above all, I am grateful to God for keeping me all the days of my life and trusting and helping me with this book.

Table of Contents

Foreword

S un Tzu is an honorific title bestowed upon Sun Wu, the author of *The Art of War*. *The Art of War* is an immensely influential ancient Chinese book on military strategy. The book teaches the reader how to fight and win.

Since at least the 1980s, *The Art of War* has been applied to fields well outside the military. Much of the text is about how to fight wars without actually having to do battle. It gives tips on how to outsmart one's opponent so that physical battle is not necessary. As such, it has found application as a training guide for many competitive endeavors that do not involve actual combat.

In the book, Tzu says, "Know the enemy and know yourself; in a hundred battles you will never peril." I am not suggesting that the male gender is the enemy of the female gender; however, the strategy still applies. If the word "enemy" is too strong, let's replace it with something that is not quite as strong. "Know the other person and know yourself; in a hundred battles you will never be defeated."

This is the point that Robert Williams makes in *Don't Hate the Player, Hate the Game: A Girl's Guide to Benching the Bad Boys.* Williams has provided a tool for the female that will help her to know the male and thereby avoid falling victim to the games that men are trained to play. This book is not only a tool for the female as she relates to the male, but it also helps the male reader to know and understand himself. Every male has at some point in time asked himself, "What makes me do the things that I do?" Williams has done an excellent job of shedding light on the male behavior.

—Bishop Jerry Hutchins
Senior Pastor, Timothy Baptist Church

Preface

Several years ago I was a part of a chaperone team from Clarke Middle School in Athens, Georgia, that carried a group of our eighth grade students to Sapelo Island, one of Georgia's barrier islands. The group's makeup consisted of some of the brightest and best students in the world. Of the twenty or more students, about half were girls.

We spent a week on the island. Their days were filled with scientific experiments, classes, writing exercises, group exploration, food preparation and of course homework. It would be late in the afternoon with the setting sun as the backdrop that the girls would share with each other their boy stories. At first, I only listened as one by one these beautiful young women shared their all-too-familiar horror tales of life with their "boyfriends." When I could not resist the need to interject anymore, I invited myself into the conversation. I gave a few words of advice to one of the girls as the others listened. I told her a little about how boys think and why most of them do the crazy things they do. She and the rest of the girls dropped everything and for the next two hours, we talked. The after-dinner talks became our nightly ritual for our week on the island. During the bus ride home, one of the girls said, "Mr. Williams, you need to write a book so all the rest of the girls out there will know what's up with these boys."

And as we know the old saying goes, the rest is history.

Come here, Kelley, Bianca, Stasha, JoEll, Jaffa, Genesis, Dreidan, and Kendra. Your uncle Bob has something he wants to tell you.

Imagine that a healthy, well-educated young man or an older, not-so-well-educated man is told that on a given stretch of beach, there is a buried treasure of immense value. He is told that the treasure is scattered over the entire clearly marked stretch of beach. The treasure consists of the most rare metals and precious stones of every kind. He is told that everything he finds he can keep for himself. He is also told that the treasure is hidden at various depths ranging from just inches beneath the surface to a few feet below the surface and that the only tools allowed in the search are a spoon and a small bucket. It is more than a safe bet that you have just started a man on a life-long search for treasure. Girls, *you* are that great treasure! You are the treasure on the beach. If he really wants to find the real you, he will dig for it for the rest of his life.

Introduction

I am a husband, the father of two sons, a brother, Uncle Bob to six nieces and ten nephews, an assistant pastor, an assistant principal, a cousin, a friend, a counselor, a godfather, and a teacher of thousands of beautiful young women. All that I say to you in this book I would say to my own little girl if I had one.

It is not my intention to bring any disharmony between the sexes, nor am I looking to level the playing field by giving up insider trading secrets. My goal is to help save a life—yours. I hope that this book will provide a platform that will serve as a launching pad for many life-changing conversations between parents and their children.

All over the world in various cultures and people groups, most boys, and even some girls, are playing a very dangerous game. The players are coached, groomed, cheered, and respected by peers and elders alike. Like many young men today, I was also coached, tutored, and groomed in the art and skill of how to play "The Game." I wish now that the game was only football, basketball, or any other sport. I was a real player, and I played to win. I was well trained in how to play the game by some of the best, most experienced players I have ever known. I was schooled in the rules and techniques of the game. I quickly learned that as long as one followed these rules, success was just a matter of time. The game plan has repeatedly worked for me and all who use it well. I have seen victim after victim fall to the techniques taught to me as a young boy growing up in the rolling hills of Bath, South Carolina, and later, on college campuses and in cities from New York to Miami. At first, I was surprised to find that the same simple rules worked just as well, if not better, on the older and supposedly more experienced females. Because of my lifelong experience with sports such as football, hunting, and fishing, I will use sports analogies extensively throughout this book to help illustrate the most important points.

As a player, I saw both sides of the game. The players and their victims can be compared to offensive and defensive players on a football team or compared to a fisherman and his prey.

Most of what I am going to say to you in the first chapters of this book will focus on the potential prey, or the offensive player. The last chapters of this book will deal with personal development and some key rules of healthy relationships. Throughout the book, I will offer readers a few of my personal quotes and those of some famous and not-so-famous people, along with definitions of the important words and terms to give us a common vocabulary, which will add to the level of understanding. The would-be players will also profit from the insights they can gain about how and why they may begin to play the game and to offer them the choice of being an old-fashion gentleman.

What's Your Problem?

It is not your fault, but it is your problem. I know that you did not make up this situation we call life. It is not your fault that, in life, sometimes bad things happen to good people. I also know that you did not ask to be born, nor did you have anything to do with starting the game that boys and so-called men play. Nevertheless, it is your problem. A problem is any situation or condition that causes you distress, difficulty, or trouble, and it is your right and/or responsibility to find a solution.

I think it is important that we understand that unless we have the right and/or the responsibility to find a solution, we do not have a genuine problem, regardless of our level of discomfort. You may not like the weather—too hot, too cool, too whatever the conditions are—but you do not have a problem with the weather, simply because it is not your responsibility or right to change it. The weather may be the *cause* of your problem, but the weather itself is not the problem. If you are cold, put on a coat. If you are too hot, find a shady spot. The discomfort caused by the weather is your real problem, not the weather. It is your right and/or responsibility to find a solution to your discomfort, not to the weather.

People are like the weather. They may cause you some problems, but they are never to be seen as the problem. It is not your right and/or responsibility to change anybody but yourself. I say this to point out the importance of the proper identification of your real problem. In life, you will find that far too many people waste a great deal of valuable time dealing with situations that they don't have the right or the responsibility to solve. I promise that just trying to live your life to the fullest will bring your fair share of problems. You will not have a shortage of them. I want to offer you three possible options to any problem you may have. They are fight, forgive, and fix. Most know how to fight, but only a few know how to fight fairly. (See "What Is the Root Cause of the Player?") In order to forgive, we must first be willing and able to give up our right to seek vengeance on those who wronged us, then to treat the guilty person as if the wrong never happened. The last option is to fix the problem. Undo the wrong; repay the loan. Settling the debt is the best way I know to move toward forgiveness.

The Water Boy

Sex is no longer a matter of your personal pleasure or a private affair. Today, because of the presence of the HIV virus and other STDs, four of which have no known cure, sex is now a matter of life and death and a worldwide concern. The HIV virus is spread from person to person almost exclusively by sexual contact.

Having sex with anyone is just like mixing two cups of water together. The contents in one cup will be thoroughly mixed with the contents of the other cup. Once mixed, there is no going back. One can never undo a sexual mixing. A person will now have in her cup whatever the sexual partner has in his cup, and vice versa. Every time a person chooses to make herself available to another partner sexually, the cups are remixed. You may be able to clear up your contents with the use of antibiotics or other treatment options, but this will not undo the fact that the sexual activity did take place.

When relating to sexually transmitted diseases (STDs), there are only two assumptions you can make about the people who you are considering as possible sexual partners. The first assumption is that the other person is clean of all STDs. Most would-be lovers almost exclusively choose this assumption. In reality, though, the second and only safe assumption is that the other person has an STD until you have current reliable test results that prove otherwise. No matter how safe the other person makes you feel, until you see test results or are willing to bet your life on that person being a virgin, you must assume he or she has an STD. I want to make this perfectly clear: I am not condoning the mixing of cups. No matter what assumption you have made, you must keep the contents of your cup to yourself. If your partner were able to present to you test results that prove that they are clean of all STDs, it would only mean that it is safe to continue to explore the possibilities of a deeper relationship.

The use of a condom does not provide you with 100% safe sex; however, the use of a latex condom will provide you with much *safer* sex. The only 100% safe sex is between two people who have kept themselves to themselves and share themselves only with each other forever. One of the major themes of this book is "choice". I have offered you my opinion, but the choice is yours. If you are going to have sex, please use a latex condom properly every time. Another major theme is "responsibility". Do not leave it up to your partner to provide a suitable condom; please take the responsibility for the provision of the condom as well as learning and teaching its proper use.

The following statements were taken from the Centers for Disease Control and Prevention (CDC) official website.

> The surest way to avoid transmission of sexually transmitted diseases is to abstain from sexual

intercourse, or to be in a long-term mutually monogamous relationship with a partner who has been tested and you know is uninfected.

For persons whose sexual behaviors place them at risk for STDs, correct and consistent use of the male latex condom can reduce the risk of STD transmission. However, no protective method is 100 percent effective, and condom use cannot guarantee absolute protection against any STD. Furthermore, condoms lubricated with spermicides are no more effective than other lubricated condoms in protecting against the transmission of HIV and other STDs. In order to achieve the protective effect of condoms, they must be used correctly and consistently. Incorrect use can lead to condom slippage or breakage, thus diminishing their protective effect. Inconsistent use, e.g., failure to use condoms with every act of intercourse, can lead to STD transmission because transmission can occur with a single act of intercourse.

While condom use has been associated with a lower risk of cervical cancer, the use of condoms should not be a substitute for routine screening with Pap smears to detect and prevent cervical cancer.

http://www.cdc.gov/condomeffectiveness/latex.htm

Knowing the Plays
Is Not Enough

Knowing the plays in the playbook is not enough to guarantee a victory. You must know and properly execute the plays to have any real chance to enjoy success. Application of knowledge is the real key to power. It is not only the quality of the knowledge but also how and when you choose to apply it that makes you truly powerful. This goes to show that knowledge is no guarantee for success. I believe that *success is the product of accurate knowledge and timely disciplined application of that knowledge; it is not the byproduct of luck and hard work.* In our modern world today, the old "D" word, discipline, is seldom ever used in reference to our lifestyle. This is what I refer to as discipline: *Discipline is the mental ability to say no to a choice now in order to say yes to a better choice later or the same choice at a better time. It is also saying yes to a choice that at the present is unpleasant or downright painful in order to enjoy a higher level of success and enjoyment later.*

Having been involved in sports most of my life as a player and later as a coach, I must confess that one of the few things that held true for me in both roles is that I hated practice, but I loved game time. More specifically, I loved to win. The only comfort I could find in practice as a player was the knowledge that it would improve my game-time performance and my chances of winning. Later as a coach, practice gave me the opportunity to get to know and help train some great young men.

I believe that a fierce competitive spirit is vital to your success in life. You may never reach your highest level of performance without it. I also believe that the most important attribute of successful people is their total unwillingness to quit.

Vince Lombardi, one of football's greatest coaches of all time, put it this way: "I firmly believe that any man's finest hour, his greatest fulfillment to all he holds dear, is that moment when he has worked his heart out in a good cause and lies exhausted on the field of battle—victorious." One of the best habits to develop as you grow into an adult is the habit of finishing what you have started.

Winning matters a lot! Whoever said, "It does not matter if you win or lose; it only matters how you play the game," must have been on or rooting for the losing team. Winning might not be everything, but it is one of the best things that life has to offer. Nobody in his or her right mind sets losing as a goal, nor does losing just happen.

Differences between Offense and Defense

Traditionally, men play the defensive role. Defensive players are trained to tune out all unnecessary noise around them. If the sound is not necessary for their immediate success, then to them it is just noise. It is like the old saying "in one ear and out the other." Offensive players, traditionally the women, are trained to move into action by a certain sound. They already know the snap count of the play, which is the predetermined sound or count that is given by the quarterback that will start the play. Men's eyes are directly connected to their hearts. If what a man sees gives him excitement, you will have his undivided attention for a play, a game, or even a season. His attention will most likely be of a sexual nature only. You do not show a "tackle-starved" defensive player the ball and expect him to think about your feelings. You must know that he is going for the fast, hard tackle. What most women hear with their ears goes directly to their hearts. That is the reason you will often see a beautiful woman walk around with a man who looks very plain or is even downright ugly—the man has found a way to get to her heart. He knows that the path to her heart is not through her eyes but her ears. He has found the right things to tell her.

All defensive players are trained to read, then react. It all starts with the formation and the position of the other team's players. A defensive player is trained to first see movement; this can be the ball or an offensive player going into motion. Next, he is to initiate contact with the offensive player, deliver a blow (cause the first physical contact), and remain engaged just long enough to read the direction of the play. Then he is to separate himself from the offensive players as quickly as possible and then run free to the ball to make the tackle. As a defensive player, he has had it drilled into his head: hit, read, separate, and run to the ball. This is the reason a man can have sex with a woman and not even know her name. It is not just because he only wants sex with her and as many other girls as he can, or that he does not care; rather, it is how he has been trained to function. Offensive players are trained to throw their entire bodies into a block—to sacrifice their body for the success of the play. The goal is to make and maintain body-to-body contact—controlling the movement of the defensive player at all times. Many women give their whole selves to a man in a relationship in an attempt to control him. Women give their hearts with every sexual encounter—if not in whole, then surely in part. For this reason, even casual sex for most women is much more than just sharing her body with a partner.

No Means No!

Y ou must show the defensive player where the line of scrimmage is. It is your job to train the man about your "No!" and your line of scrimmage. For the most part, the law of the land and our court system deals with what is out of bounds. Perhaps all of his life, a male has been dealing with females whose *no* may have meant "Not now" or "Not here." His mother, grandmother, sister, teachers, and ex-girlfriends may have trained him that "no" does not always mean "no." The best time for you to do this training is very early in the relationship, right from the very beginning—the first snap of the first game of the season. From the first conversation, you are setting and establishing the ground rules for the relationship. You must be clear about your expectations for the relationship. At this time, you may or may not share your expectations with him, but it is best that you are clear about them just the same. You must expect him to test your determination, to see if your no means no. You must pass this test.

Most women do not want a man who is smaller, weaker, slower, younger, less experienced, or with fewer resources than themselves. Most women want a man whom they can look up to. What most women want in a man is someone who is bigger, stronger, faster, older, more experienced, and with more resources than themselves. If you are alone with this type of male who has not learned that your "no" means "no," you could be putting your very life in danger.

We live in a world where we are expected to have and maintain numerous relationships. The reality of the matter is that all relationships are subject to some level of outside accountability. Being accountable means being subject to giving a response for actions taken in the performance of prescribed duties or tasks. No matter what the relationship is or how long it has survived, all parties are accountable to the law of the land. A woman may be a wife of ten years, but she cannot do whatever she feels like doing to her husband just because they are married. For example, if she is angry with him, she cannot shoot him, cut him, or even hit him just because they are married.

The offensive player must have a male on her side of the line of scrimmage acting as a line judge—a father figure in her life to hold her male friend accountable to him (the father/father figure) in the relationship. The line of scrimmage is an imaginary plane that starts at the front tip of the ball and extends straight up into infinity and from sideline to sideline. Both sides of the ball must respect the line of scrimmage. If a defensive player breaks this plane before the ball is moved by the offensive team, the player will be called off sides by the line judge and then the defensive team will be penalized five yards. Jumping off sides can become a habit by repeating the behavior, and yet few would argue that this is an activity that players should perfect because it makes your defensive team move back five yards and the offensive team back up ten yards, which is not the direction the team wants to go. Accountability can only exist in a relationship where it is enforced. Even after the marriage, you need the protection and covering of a father at all times in a relationship. Though this may be old-fashioned and outdated according to today's standards, it is a time-tested, tried and true lifesaver. I promise you that he will treat you much better if he knows that he will have to answer to the other man/men in your life for any mistreatment of you. A brother figure would be less effective, but it is much better than no male figure at all.

There must be internal as well as external accountability if the relationship is to have any real chance of being a successful one. Internal accountability is the mutual accountability shared between the people in the relationship. This accountability is the lifeblood of every successful relationship. Without it, the relationship is in constant danger of the ills of human weakness. Unless both parties are mutually accountable to each other, it is just a matter of time before one or both will abuse the relationship. Without outside accountability, the relationship will be very isolated from the rest of the world. At first glance, this may look desirable, but look a little deeper past the surface and see how shallow and potentially dangerous such a relationship would really be.

In any relationship, it is very important that only behaviors one wishes to be repeated are supported and/or tolerated. For example, if you do not want him to ever curse at you, do not allow him to use that kind of language in your presence. If you allow him to use profanity around you, it is just a matter of time before he uses it on you. If you do not want to become his tackling bag, do not ever allow him to hit you—not even in play. When a line is crossed, blow the whistle. Bring everything to a stop, and deal with the issue immediately on the spot. Now this means that you must also model only acceptable behavior at all times. After all, he deserves to get as well as he gives. Let me share the advice my father gave me as a boy growing into manhood: "People are going to treat you the way you let them." You must take responsibility for what you allow people to get away with. Allow me to add this piece of advice: never let anybody do anything to you that you would not do to yourself. For example, if you are not beating on yourself, do not let anybody else do it. Another one of my favorite Coach Vince Lombardi sayings is, "Practice makes only permanent; only perfect practice makes perfect and permanent." This means that to repeat any behavior will only make that behavior a habit.

Rules of the Game

As a young man growing up under the tutelage of my uncles and older cousins, I learned the basic rules of the game, which are straightforward and simple. There are only two foundational rules, and they form the basis on which the entire game is played out. There may be many different variations on how they are expressed, but I believe that the sentiments are the same.

The first rule: If you are going to be a player, you cannot care; and if you are going to care, you cannot be a player. The value and contribution of the first rule is that it gives the player a sense of invincibility. In any given situation, if you are not scared of the worst thing that could happen to you, one of the natural responses is to develop an edged confidence that borders on arrogance. In sports, this attitude is often called swagger. Many women and girls find it irresistible. The second rule: Keep the girls out of your heart and far apart and you will never be alone, night or day. The heart and soul of the second rule is not to break the first rule. Problems arise only when the would-be player either does not know the rules or attempts to break them. If you have decided that you want to be a player, you have also decided that you will live a life void of lasting, meaningful relationships with the opposite sex. People who are committed to playing the game are committed to shallow, temporary interactions, not long-lasting, genuine, and productive relationships.

Fishing: Three Keys to a Successful Outing

I have been fishing all of my life, and over the years I have caught thousands of fish. I have read books and have spent thousands of dollars on fishing equipment. I have watched untold hours of fishing programs and videos. I have spent days shopping for the right tackle. Through my experience, I have learned that there are three basic keys to catching any species of fish in any condition on any given day. They are

• Go where the fish are
• Show the fish what they want to see
• Present that bait to the fish the way they want to see it

The ultimate goal of the fisherman is not to catch the fish but to get the fish to catch him.

Now what does all of this fishing stuff have to do with the game? These are the same three keys to catching a female.

The first and most important key is to go where the fish are, not just to the water, but to the place on the water where the fish are and the depth that the fish are.

I know this sounds simple, but after all, simplicity is the goal here. Every fish species has its favorite habitat for a given season, weather, and water condition. The experienced fisherman knows that the fish are not in every part of the lake or pond. In addition, a particular habitat will attract a particular type of fish in a particular season. No doubt, men have learned that there are certain places where certain types of females hang out. If a man had in mind to find a health-conscious female, it is off to the gym. For a nature lover, it is off to the park. If he wants a spiritual girl, well, then he heads off to church.

Key two is to show the fish what they want to see. Use the right prey item. What are the fish feeding on? The most successful fisherman and players are very adept at lure selection. The trick is observation. Take note of what the fish are feeding on and then match the lure as best you can to the desired prey item. To find out what a woman wants, just look at what she has or has recently had. Real players know that it is not what a woman *says* that she wants but what a woman settles for that really counts. A female might say she wants a well-educated man with a lot of style, but if she is repeatedly drawn into relationships with roughnecks and thugs, you will find that the experienced player will approach her as a roughneck or a thug.

Key three is to show the fish the prey item the way they want to see it. Master fishermen not only have a wide variety of lures at their disposal, but they have also mastered a number of different deadly presentations for each lure. Most females want a man with money, right? The question now becomes, "What kind of man is he with his money?" Is she looking for a high roller or the quiet and discreet man? Physically fit, yes, but does she want the joke of the day or the brooding philosopher?

Location, lure selection, and presentation are the three keys to any successful outing for an angler or a player. I say all of this to let you know that they are out there looking for you. Now you must decide whether you are going to be this season's trophy keeper, catch of the day, or the one who never bit and lived.

A Player's Three F's

Real players live by the three F's.

F1: Find them. For a few players, it is all about the chase. The thrill of the hunt drives them to the chase after the would-be victim. These players may call it quits as soon as the chase is over. A few may not enter into a sexual relationship with the captured prey. If they choose to have sex, it will most often be a one-night stand. Like a big cat that gives chase solely because the prey runs, these players are thrill seekers.

F2: Flag them. For most hardened and seasoned players of the game, sex is the least they want for their investment of time. Clothes, cars, money, and a place to live are all a part of "staking the flag." More than a few women have found themselves broke, busted, and disgusted after falling victim to a real player.

F3: Forget about them. In order for the player to continue his personal rampage through the lives of other victims, he must forget about all past victims and conquests. As a player, one cannot afford the burden of a guilty conscience. A guilty conscience and a player's mentality are like noise and silence: the more you have of one the less you have of the other. One must remember that players are people in transition. Most transition through the player stage completely; others seem to be stuck for much longer. When dealing with a male player, you must remember that there is no difference between him and a boy. You must understand that boys come in all ages. Age has very little, if anything, to do with manhood. You can be a fifty-one-year-old boy or a fifteen-year-old man. The old saying that age is just a number is remarkably true when it comes to players and manhood.

It is vital that you recognize the fact that there is a night-and-day difference between men and boys. I know that this next statement is very generalizing, and it seems to group all boys negatively, but take it for what it is: my personal opinion based on my life experience and observation. The number one thing you must know about all boys is that they will always, always, always play games. Boys live to play games. Any game will do. Girls become just another part of the games they play. That is why they will often refer to females as "play things." If a boy is successful in having sex with a girl, he has "scored."

If you choose to become involved with a *boy*, know that he can and will only *play* with you. As a boy, he is not capable of being serious for any real length of time. After all, a boy is, by definition, an immature male child. To play with boys is to play with fire. It is not a matter of whether you are going to be burned; it is just a matter of when and how badly you will be burned.

Know this: there is a little boy in every man, and a little man in every boy. Do not be fooled by the little man in him into thinking that he is all man, mostly man, or even a man at all. At the same time, do not let the little boy in him turn you off to perhaps developing a relationship with a real man.

Not All Males Are Players, But All Have the Potential

Many of you may be wondering how a male can be a diehard player for so many years and then settle down to life with a single woman. There is much to be said about the maturity level he has reached, but it has been my experience that the biggest factor in the start and development of his new monogamous lifestyle is the caliber of woman he is dealing with. I am aware that such a statement puts a lot of responsibility on the female. Remember that where there is responsibility there is also the authority. You need to make sure that the relationship proceeds at your pace and in the direction you desire. The female must take responsibility for the quality of the relationship from day one. If she defers this responsibility to the male, then she has set herself up as a helpless victim, totally dependent upon his whims for the life of the relationship. You will be forced to play the role of a terminator instead of a thermostat in the relationship; you will be forced to kill the relationship after you have suffered who knows what at his hands. Every time you allow him to mistreat you, you have just allowed him to reset your line of scrimmage in his favor.

It is important to understand that no one can look at a male and determine whether or not he is a player. What happens most often is that the woman relies on her own past experiences or the advice of some other female. The danger in this situation is obvious. If the female has had little or no experience, she may find herself a helpless victim in the hands of an experienced player. Even females with a great deal of experience in dealing with players may find themselves overconfident, thus making themselves as likely a victim as the inexperienced. The only safeguard from being the next victim is to recognize the fact that all males have the potential to be a player. Once again, perhaps the most important factor that will determine whether a male will play or stay is not the player; it is the caliber of woman with whom he is dealing.

Real players are students of human nature. They can read a smile, a nervous cough, and the slightest hesitation as though they were words written on paper. To a player, desperation in a female's behavior is like blood in the water to a shark. Many players and all dogs live for the easy kill. There is a lot to the old saying, "Never let them see you sweat." For this reason, I offer some simple advice: never play games with a player; you will always lose. There are things in this life you should never waste time doing. Never waste your time arguing with a fool, because it takes a fool to argue with a fool. Never take the time to track down a rumor; all you will find is trouble. And never waste time playing games with a player; you will always lose.

Players Come in a Variety of Styles

Before we tackle this subject, there is another type of male I want to talk about. This is your pleasure-seeking dog, often misnamed as a player. The dog is a straight sex fanatic who seeks sexual pleasure for pleasure's sake. The true dog does not have standards of any kind. He chooses his sexual partners by one simple criterion: If she is here and willing, then she is the one for now. If you ask a dog why he had sex with his last partner, do not be at all surprised when the response is, "She was there." The motto of the dog is, "From eight to eighty, blind, lame, crippled, or crazy." This means that to the dog, it does not matter who the sexual partner is. Anybody's body will do.

I want to share with you three broad types of players. From the birth of human history, man has occupied three major roles as the provider for the family unit: herdsman, hunter, and hunter-gatherer. I will use these same broad categories to identify players.

The *herdsmen* are after the timid, docile, tamed, settled females who often have low self-esteem. The herdsman prefers to gather and maintain a herd of females.

39

This type of player prides himself on the sheer number of females he has gathered rather than their individual quality. However, the herdsman does have minimum standards of admittance. The herdsman would prefer to share himself with a stable of ten females he rates as sevens on a scale of one to ten, as opposed to having one or two tens. When remarking about his love life, he most often will mention the number of females he is currently "running" (playing the game on) or is involved with sexually. The motto of the herdsman is, "The more, the merrier."

The *hunter* is after the wild, independent, free-roaming female with a projected high self-esteem. The hunter enjoys the hunt. For him it is the sheer thrill of the chase that he hungers for. The hunter is always looking for the trophy. Once the hunter has bagged his prey and displayed her to all of his friends, he is quick to lay her aside and start the hunt all over again, this time for a fresh new victim. The hunter lives by the three F's as his motto (Find them, Flag them, and Forget about them).

The *hunter-gatherer* has the widest range of potential victims when it comes to the type of female he is after. The hunter-gatherer has the run of the field. He is just as comfortable with the timid sheep as he is giving chase to the wild doe. The hunter-gatherer's motto is, "If you can't be with the one you love, then love the one you are with."

What Dating a Player Can Teach You about Yourself

Of all the things you will learn from dating a player, perhaps the most important is that you are a survivor. If you have fallen victim to the game of a player, first, remember you are still alive. Yes, there is life after being played. Countless females can back me up on this one. Just ask the next woman you meet. Chances are that she is the survivor of an encounter with a player. Learn and grow from the experience. You are a lot tougher than you ever knew.

A second lesson that dating a player may teach you about yourself is that you should trust yourself more. Somewhere deep down inside, you knew that he was a player. You heard a small voice telling you that something was wrong with this relationship, but you were too afraid to cut your losses and walk away. That is why you felt even worse after you learned the whole truth.

The third lesson learned is to appreciate the rare and unique gift you are to the world and to any man's life. A word of caution: never give in to drinking from the poisonous cup of comparison. It will always kill your personal development. Every day of your life, you are offered the cup of comparison through hundreds of commercial advertisements. Most advertisements have one specific goal—to create a need in you. If they can get you to make a comparison between you, who does not have their product, and their person, who does have it, and get you to see yourself as lacking what they are selling, then it is just a matter of time before the product is sold. They made the sale as soon as a comparison was made. When you compare yourself to anyone else, you move down the path of self-destruction. When I use the term self-destruction, I am not talking about suicide. I am talking about the destruction of your unique personality.

Just picture the most handsome young man or woman you could ever dream of, with the sweetest personality to go along with a body like Usher's or Beyonce's. Now, imagine, what if every young man or woman in the world was identical in every way to your dream guy or girl. How long would it take you to get sick of that face and that wonderful personality? While attending college, I took a microeconomics course, and one of the many things I learned from the course was the law of supply and demand. Simply stated, if the supply is low and the demand is high, the price will be high. When supply is high and the demand is low, the price will be low. Throughout history and especially now, the demand for quality, intelligent females is very high.

So, how do you get out of this entire meat-grinding situation now? Simple—change your mind. Change your attitude about you and others around you. You are not for sale to the man willing to meet your price, nor is there an auction, in which you are on sale to the highest bidder. Real diamonds do not seek; they are sought. You have never seen a diamond walking around looking for a man to whom it may sell itself. Diamonds are just diamonds. Men seek them out for their beauty and glory. There is a certain glory attached to the most rare and beautiful things around us. In this world, there are a great number of beautiful things all around us, but it is the combination of beauty, rarity, and difficulty to obtain that boosts the price of precious stones. Why do I take the time to tell you all this? The answer is simple. You must decide if you want to be a diamond or just a lump of coal. It is your personal choice. It is far too important to leave to anyone else.

What Is the Root Cause of the Player?

On the surface, it may seem that the dog and the player are one in the same. However, you should dare to look deeper to see what really motivates a player to be a player.

Pain is one of the chief ways our anger is revealed. Pain exposes then feeds our anger. Today, anger is culturally acceptable and expected. It is strange to me that if we meet a happy person, we want to know what is wrong with them. We never think that it might be what is right with them and what is wrong with us. Your anger is a real, natural emotion. The pain caused by attempts to take away from our personal self-worth will fuel our anger. The conflict that arises because of any effort to change our attitudes and basic thought patterns will also feed our anger. To sum it all up, anytime we do not get what we think, need, want, or deserve, the result is fuel for our anger. Anger and pain are like a lit pilot light in a gas heater; they all have one. Anger is a small flame that goes unnoticed until the thermostat triggers the gas/pain. The gas hits the pilot light, then the entire house will feel heat from it.

The genesis of the player is pain. The player has simply chosen an anesthesia to ease his pain. We all have a wide selection of pain blockers available to us. We can try playing our pain away, drinking and drugging, having sex, going shopping, eating in extremes (overeating or starving oneself), going to parties, clubs, or church.

The list of pain blockers includes most of our self-destructive behaviors ranging from denial to suicide. No matter what pain blocker we choose, the pain is still there waiting on us to deal with it. Somewhere in the player's life there are emotional scars that may have been caused by the shame and pain of rejection, betrayal or even abuse. Many players are motivated by the thrill of controlling other people's lives. This is often an attempt to counter and overcompensate for the lack of control in their own lives. However, the motivation for most players is revenge.

When I look back over my life, it is easy for me to remember the painful event that launched me into my playing days. It was my senior year in high school. I was living a dream life. I was one of the top players on my high school football team and a decent basketball player. A solid student in the classroom, I had exceeded the NCAA required score on the SAT and was offered a football scholarship by Chowan Junior College in North Carolina. To top it all off, I was in love. My heart was hers. She was my first real love. There was very little on earth I would not have done for that girl. Shortly after my hometown newspaper reported my college offer and my acceptance, I got a call from my girlfriend. She told me that we were over. She said that I would leave home and meet another girl at college. Standing six feet tall and weighing almost 200 pounds, I am not ashamed to say that it felt like she ripped a gaping hole in my chest. I was humbled to my knees by a girl who stood five feet, four inches tall and weighed 125 pounds. I found myself begging her not to do that to us. To say that I was hurt would be a great disservice to my pain. I had never suffered that kind of pain before in my life and never since. Over the next several months, as I struggled with my loss, my life slowly came back into some kind of order, but I was never the same. I was damaged goods. I was changed, and it was not for the better. In my pain, I made a solemn promise to myself that I would never let that happen to me again. I would never care about anybody enough that I could hurt like that ever again. I would never cry about another girl in my life. "The next time tears fall, they won't be mine," I promised. It was a promise I kept for many years, even into my marriage.

To add to my struggles, my father died over the Christmas break of my first year of college. I felt very helpless and out of control again. With all my strength and athletic ability, I could not stop people from leaving me. Up to this point, I had only listened to the lessons of my tutors in the game with passive interest. Now motivated by my pain, I sought revenge, and to regain a sense of control back in my life, I put into practice every lesson taught to me about the game. I even made up some along the way. This was the start of my personal rampage through the lives of far too many young women to accurately recount.

Your anger is not a choice, but your response to your anger is. You can never manage your anger until you first manage your response to your anger. Your anger demands expression. Most people have never taken an anger-management class, so allow me give you one in a nutshell. To manage your anger is to manage your choice of expression, not the anger itself. Remember what we said about problems? Your real problem is not the anger but your chosen expression of the anger. It is unrealistic to say to yourself that you will never allow anything or anyone to make you angry for the rest of your life. It is, however, well within your ability to make and keep the following promise to yourself: "The next time I am angry, I will choose an appropriate expression of my anger."

There are countless ways to express your anger. I want to ignore all of the negative expressions and instead focus on a three-step plan you can use to help rid yourself of all of your anger from the past and then help you more effectively manage your expression of anger in the future.

Admit your anger to yourself. If someone caused you pain and anger that springs from that pain, simply say to yourself, "I am hurt and angry." Do not deny your anger.

Admit it to the person who caused you the anger. This confession should not be the cause of another conflict. You must be respectful, calm, clear, and honest. I suggest a technique called triangulation. By using this method of discussing issues, the focus of the discussion is on the issue and never you or the other person.

To utilize triangulation, be ready to express to the other person specifically what action/behavior they took that caused your pain. Know that the focus has to be on the action or behavior, not the person. By doing this, defensive walls can be kept lowered. I agree with author Steven Covey when he says that the first task in communication is that you seek to understand, then you may seek to be understood. Remember, you must keep the issue, you, and the other person separate. The other person is never the issue or the problem. To think otherwise is a recipe for disaster. If you allow your thinking to focus on the other person, then the only way to get rid of your issue or problem permanently is to get rid of the other person permanently. The law tends not to be in favor of the results of this kind of thinking.

Drop it. I am well aware that this is much easier said than done. I do not know what people may have done to you or how many times they did it, but I have one question for you: How long are you going to carry around that pain and anger? What else can you do with it? Soul singer Roberta Flack had this to say about painful situations, "The situation you live in doesn't have to live in you." This might be the hardest thing you have ever done or will do in your life, but I promise you that the freedom and relief you will gain is well worth the effort.

The Ultimate Victim of Every Player Is the Player

The player always loses out in the end. For the diehard player, there is only a lonely life of selfishness and endless pain. The player will never know the depth and comfort of a meaningful, personal relationship with the opposite sex. The old player is harmless because you can see him coming from miles away. He is pitiful because he is still out there long after all the other players of his day have either transitioned to more mature relationships or died. The old player will live out his last days in lonely isolation, laughed at by those far younger than he is. No matter how grand his old titles were, all over-the-hill players end up with the same title: Old Fool.

When the player is ready to leave, nothing at all can make him stay. Even if you somehow manage to keep his body, his heart is elsewhere. The best thing you can do for yourself when dealing with a player with happy feet is to let him run. Cut your losses, learn from the experience, and live on. It is my observation that success is the highest and purest form of revenge. There are no laws against it, and the ones you love the most will benefit as well. Success is far more than the destination or a finished product; it is the journey of life itself. Every day you are alive is another important step in your journey of success. As you live your life in the pursuit of success, you must balance this with the insight that where you are right now is a success. On your journey, you are going to make some mistakes and some stupid choices. Your major task is to learn from them both and keep moving.

David Brinkley, a noted news anchor and personality, once said, "A successful man is one who can lay a firm foundation with the bricks others have thrown at them." After your success, the player will end up singing that old hit song by the O'Jay's, "She Used to be My Girl."

Who Are You?

I mean, who are you really? What are you really about? Before you can truly share yourself with someone else, you must first be aware of who and what you are sharing. One of the real problems with relationships is that either one or both parties is ignorant about who he or she really is. Who you really are has everything to do with who and what it will take to have a successful relationship. You must know who you are in order to know what you bring to the table. Far too many people think too little of themselves to see themselves as an asset in a relationship. It is very important that you should be able to list the majority of your many assets. If not all, surely you should be able to pick your top ten. There are a number of self-administered, personal inventories available today, any of which will start you down the exciting road of personal self-discovery. You must learn to be content with the real you. You are a person who just happened to be born a female or a male. Contentment is the result of personally recognizing and accepting the truth that your life is far better than you deserve.

No matter your life situation, you do not need to look far to find a crowd of people who would gladly take your place. I mean, if they knew everything—all of it, every ugly little detail—they would still jump at the chance to trade places with you. Even if they had a list of all your disabilities, shortcomings, and failures, they would still want to be you.

Most people seem to think that the grass is greener on the other side of the fence. Few such thinkers ever consider the fact that if they take the time to water their own grass, it too would be greener. Contentment, more than anything else, is a part of the successful attitude you must develop. My definition of attitude is a simple one: *Attitude is your chosen, basic outlook on life. It is the way you decide to see people, events, and the stages of life.*

The key word in the definition of attitude is *chosen.* "*The last of the human freedoms is to choose one's attitude in any given circumstances,*" said Victor Frankl, survivor of a Nazi concentration camp during WWII. If you choose, you can make every day the best day of your life. So, you want to know how you can make this wonderful thing called contentment happen in your life? It is as simple as one, two, three, and four.

The first step is the easiest of the four because you must accept the fact that no matter what you do, you cannot go back to yesterday and change it. There are no do-overs. Step two is very much the same. No matter what you do, you cannot go ahead to tomorrow. The third step is to accept the fact that all you have is today because you cannot go back nor go ahead. Today has to be the best day of your life because it is the only real day you have to live.

As important as yesterday was and tomorrow will be, today is far more important. Yesterday is a dim, fading memory of what was. Tomorrow is an unclear, uncertain image of what may be. Only today is real enough for us to live in. Yes, you are to remember the past. Yes, you are to make plans for the future, but do not forget to live today. Live your life to the fullest today. Live like today will be your last day because one day sooner than you might believe, it will be.

The fourth step is the fuel source for your new attitude on life. If you can take it as a fact that one day you are going to die, then you are very close to a fresh, new mind-set. The day that you are going to die is coming closer every day you live. Every day of life brings us closer to that last day because you did not die yesterday, and that only increases the chance that it will happen today. Use this knowledge as fuel for your passion for life and love. Please hear me; I am not saying go out and set yourself and the world on fire and go out in a blaze of glory, nor am I saying you should sit around crying about the fact that this could be your last day alive. What I am saying is live a life of balance. Do not merely be alive, but live. Enjoy today as if it is the last spoonful of your favorite ice cream in the bowl, but remember that you might be able to get seconds.

Do You Really Want to Be Great?

I have two rules to offer you that can start you on the road toward real greatness if you can accept and allow them to help shape and frame your attitude. Every great man and woman in the present and throughout history has lived a life consistent with these two rules. The first rule: 99% of the time life is not about you. The second rule: 99% of the time life is not about now.

Before you can start your personal development into greatness, you have a very important choice to make about your life: do you want to just be ordinary or do you want to be great? You must come to grips with this next statement. If you are good to only you, then you are no good to the rest of us.

Rule 1: I know that your videos, music, friends, culture, and family have been telling you all your life that this is your world and that you are sharing it with the rest of us. Do not take the rain personally. Some people take themselves and their lives so personally that if it rains, they think that it is raining on them. Back up and chill. It may be raining, but just look around you; you are not the only one getting wet. Most of us live our lives doing what we do, constantly asking ourselves, "What's in it for me?" We never ask the question, "How can I help someone else solely for his or her benefit?" Ask yourself this question: How will my life make this world a better place? The greater the difference, the greater your life will be. No difference equals no greatness.

Rule 2: Most of the time, we believe life is to be lived for the here and now. Seldom do we really give serious thought about how our tomorrow can be negatively impacted by what we do today. What you put into your body today might not kill you today, but it may kill you tomorrow. Remember that the key here—and in life—is balance. All of the best things in life will keep. You do not need to be in a big rush to do all of your growing up today. The world will wait on you. Anything and anybody that cannot wait on you now will only end up leaving you later. If you are going to get left behind one day anyway, why not let that person leave you before you invest your time and heart in the situation in the first place?

In many ways, life is like eating your favorite ice cream. You enjoy each scoop, slowly taking down every sweet drop on a hot summer day, never satisfying your stomach but enjoying every bit of the effort. You are content with where you are in your enjoyment of the bowl, but not satisfied. You are driven by sheer delight to reach for the next spoonful to see what new sweetness it will bring. Why would anybody mess up a great dessert by rushing to the end just because they want to get there right now? (I do not even want to talk about brain freeze!)

Who Are You Working on Becoming?

There is an old saying that says, "Good things come to those who wait." I offer this variation: "Good things come to those who work long and well." Life is to be lived, not viewed as a spectator. Prince Charming came looking for Cinderella only after she took it upon herself to go to the dance. You must be willing to be a part of your process of change. If who you are now is not who you want to be five years from now, and if what you are doing now is not what you want to be doing five years from now, the question now is: what are you doing to change you? Whatever the difference is now, it must be eliminated if the new you will become a reality. You must take an active part in the process of eliminating the difference between the two. You must go to school, save the money, lose the weight, start the business, learn to skydive, or whatever your goal may be. The legendary football coach Vince Lombardi once said, "The dictionary is the only place that success comes before work. Hard work is the price we must pay for success. I think you can accomplish anything if you're willing to pay the price."

The trick is that there is no trick. Make a plan, stick

to it, and work toward the goal. Work on you like your life depends on it, because it does.

Too Old for Boys, But Too Young for a Man: What Is a Girl to Do?

I hope that this entire book will be a great help for all my daughters and sisters across all ages, ethnic groups and geographic boundaries. In this section, however, I want to speak especially to my younger daughters, those as young as eight years of age. Take the time to grow yourself as a person before you share with someone else that which is too weak to survive on its own. The real you, from the ages of nine to seventeen, is just too weak and underdeveloped to share with anyone else at this time. I am not talking about how you fill out your jeans and your halter tops; you may have all the curves and swerves to get any man's undivided attention for a moment. However, remember, it is his undivided love and respect you must have. While I am on the subject of clothes, I might as well tell you that what you choose to put on your body tells a player a lot about what is going on inside of your head. You might have an "apple bottom," but you do not need to show it to the world. If he sees you dressed in tight, revealing clothes, he sees a *body* crying for his attention. Notice I said he sees a *body,* not a person. Walking around wearing a halter top, low-cut hip huggers that show your underwear, or tight pants or shorts with words written across the bottoms calls attention to only your body, not the treasure you really are. Showing your belly button always drops his mind and attention to a place it needn't be. Cleavage draws the dogs in for the cheap thrill and the easy kill. One of my many tasks at Clarke Middle School is to chaperone after-school dances. Many of the dance moves I see little girls making on the middle school dance floor today are the same ones I saw strippers doing on tabletops and in lap dances in strip clubs when I was in my younger, wilder days. If you are all about the style of wearing fewer, tighter, and shorter clothes to get more attention like a hip-hop video honey, he will be right there with you until you peel off the last string of clothing and the last sensation is enjoyed. However, do not look for him after the freak show is over; he will be long gone seeking the next freak.

One of the most important questions you must ask, and be sure of the answer, is, "What does he really want from me?" Does he want *you* or does he want *it?* There is a night-and-day difference between the two. You cannot shy away from this question. If it is you he wants, sex should not be a part of the relationship before marriage. If sex is all or a major part of what he wants from you, you must have the character to say no to settling for just a physical-based relationship with no real hope for a future. If all he sees is your face, the size of your hips, the curve of your thighs, the shape of your butt, or the length of your hair, he has not seen you yet. The real you is hidden deeper than that. Remember that you're the treasure on the beach. It is the real you he must seek.

An eagle is not an eagle because it has the right family. Eagles are far more than what hatches from the egg; they are the product of great effort. Yes, eagles are the results of purposeful effort. The eagle chicks are taught from their very first bite that they are different from all other birds and animals. From its first taste of flesh, the baby eagle is fed a variety of meats to form a well-balanced diet. Their diet consists of rabbits, fish, birds, squirrels, snakes, and even other birds of prey. Raising eagles is hard and important work—so important that only eagles and certified professionals can legally touch a baby eagle.

Anyone can touch a chicken, but only a select few will ever have the privilege of touching an eagle. Why settle for being just a chicken when you can choose to be an eagle? You say, "My grandmother was a chicken and my mother was a chicken and now I'm a chicken." Do not let your confusion about the difference between facts and truths hinder your transformation. Facts change every day, but truth is eternal. The facts in your situation may be based on reality, but the truth is never based on anything but truth. The fact is you are who you are now. The truth of the matter is that you can be so much more. Look at your watch. What time is it? The time on your watch is a fact based on the reality of time. However, you know that in just one minute the fact of the correct time will change; it must change. Remember that truth is eternal and can only be based on that which is eternal. I offer you this truth: you can become far greater than you are.

There are many great vehicles for preparation and personal development available to you today, but they all take time. Going to college, obtaining some form of higher education, enlisting in the military, entering the workforce, or developing a business will all aid in your enhancement as a strong person.

Examples of the Gap

I want to give you some reasons why I think girls should wait to get involved in exclusive relationships. In my opinion, the age difference of five to seven years is a great one. If you are eleven, he is sixteen to eighteen. If you are twelve, he is seventeen to nineteen. A relationship of any sexual nature at this time should end with your lover in jail on child molestation charges. Nevertheless, not all is lost. Let us continue with the math.

- You are thirteen; he is eighteen to twenty.
- You are fourteen; he is nineteen to twenty-one.
- You are fifteen; he is twenty to twenty-two.
- You are sixteen; he is twenty-one to twenty-three.
- You are seventeen; he is twenty-two to twenty-four.
- You are eighteen; he is twenty-three to twenty-five.
- You are nineteen; he is twenty-four to twenty-six.
- You are twenty; he is twenty-five to twenty-seven.
- You are twenty-one; he is twenty-six to twenty-eight.
- You are twenty-two; he is twenty-seven to twenty-nine.
- You are twenty-three; he is twenty-eight to thirty.

- You are twenty-four; he is twenty-nine to thirty-one.
- You are twenty-five; he is thirty to thirty-two.
- You are thirty; he is thirty-five to thirty-seven.
- You are thirty-five; he is forty to forty-two.
- You are fifty; he is fifty-five to fifty-seven.

As time passes, the five-to-seven-year gap works in your favor. The five to seven years also gives him time to get ready for you as well. Who wants to settle for less when they could have so much more? Remember the "D" word (discipline). When you are eleven, he is sixteen to eighteen. That puts him in high school or in his freshman year in college, boot camp, or entry level in a career. He is learning the life lessons that will provide a large part of the foundation of his confidence—confidence that will one day mean so much to you.

You are "sweet sixteen," and he is now twenty-one to twenty-three. He is now some five years in the military life. He has thousands of miles under his belt and many adventures and stories to share with you. He is in his senior year in college, working at a co-op, and looking forward to launching out into a career. Now he is negotiating for his second big raise or moving to a supervisory position. He has formed his first private business venture.

You are twenty-one; he is twenty-six to twenty-eight. He has settled into his vocation. He now has life goals that call for a life-long partner. By now, he has laughed at enough jokes by himself. He has eaten enough meals alone. He now realizes—more than ever before—that it is not good for him to be alone. If you are willing to wait, you get a man who is a better companion, who has more, and who is more willing to share all he is and has with you.

Who Wants to Be a Cheater or Be Cheated?

Another reason to wait is not to cheat him or yourself out of a wonderful gift. Wait for him and do not cheat him out of one of your most precious jewels. As far as cheating him, I cannot express to you in words the deep desire of most men to be the first and only lover a woman ever has. Virginity is a subject that is talked about very little today. Therefore, I will say it to you. It is a most precious gift. Its value exceeds clothes, cars, and cruises. We are all born with only the one virginity to share with one person, and once you give it away or even if it is stolen away from you, it is gone forever; you can never get it back. Your virginity is one of the most precious and rare things. You are not to trade it for anything but only give it as a gift in exchange for a lifelong commitment. If I have not spelled it out plainly enough, I support abstinence until after the negative results of the HIV/STD tests and marriage. (Test, marriage, then sex—in that order.)

Now here is a good place for us to agree on a definition of abstinence. By abstinence I mean no physical contact of any kind that has the intended purpose of giving or receiving pleasure of a sexual nature. I strongly recommend two different HIV/AIDS tests at least a year apart. The first test should come immediately after the engagement and the second about three months before the marriage. If he objects to the test and refuses them, end the relationship. You must remember the cups of water that we talked about in the earlier pages of this book. This is a matter of life and death—yours.

If the one you are with now is not the one, then you are cheating yourself and the one who is.

The fact is that there are thousands of people in this world that you can make a relationship work with—at least for a while. However, I know that the dream of every woman and man is to meet "the one"—the one with whom you want to build and invest the rest of your life. When one considers the total population of the world, the United States, your state, city, or town, the chances of meeting the one becomes almost a mathematical impossibility. In light of this information, no wonder many people are leaving the whole thing up to chance or turning to the hot new trend of online dating firms and chat rooms. I think the most important step to make is to first discover who and what you want to be, then begin the process of becoming that new you before you seek to have a serious relationship.

I believe that the right *type* of person should get more attention from you than the right person. The right type of person will be the type who appreciates you for who you are now and who is willing and able to assist you in the process of becoming the new and better you. No matter if you believe that people come together because they are made for each other or bump into each other by dumb chance, the fact is that people do find each other. Some of us find and are found much more often than others are. Let us assume that you are now a part of a couple and you know that the relationship is a dead end. You are cheating yourself out of very important preparation time. Every second you waste in a dead-end relationship cheats you, not to mention the exposure to health and psychological risks. If it is a dead end, let it end now.

The Value of the Time Test

You can use the time test to help you evaluate the quality of all of your relationships. The time test is just that—time. Give it time to see what is growing. Do not ever allow anyone else to tell you how much time is enough time for you—especially him. Let me emphasize what I think is the only period for having sex. Any time after you and he say, "I do" in a legal ceremony, then you should have sex as often as you both like. This is, of course, after the two negative results on the HIV/STD tests. Timing is vital to success in almost every venture in life. Timing is not everything, but it may be all you have. The fact that you have said no and meant no may be the only thing that makes you stand out from the crowd. The timing of sharing yourself with another person is vital to your survival and the success of the relationship.

Do not trust too soon. You do not pass out your trust as if it were your phone number. People must earn your trust over time. You are to trust the other person only after you have shared a history of positive experiences. Most women trust far too soon with far too little reason. What reason has he given you to trust him with your very life? In addition, when I say time, I do not mean two weeks, two months, or even two years. Once again, remember the treasure on the beach analogy used earlier. Make the brother dig, sister! I remember a report I saw on television a few years ago about a couple engaged to be married. The groom had reportedly spent $1 million on the wedding, reception, and the honeymoon. When the costly day finally arrived, he stood her up. He walked away, leaving her on the "happiest" day of her life—a paid vacation but no husband. Remember, "I do" first!

As a former math teacher, I want to offer you this equation to remember: Trust–Reason = Stupidity.

I May Want You, But
I Don't Need You

You may want him, but you do not *have* to have him. One of life's greatest lessons is learning who and what you can live without. Let us think for just one second here. If you had to have him to live, how have you lived this long without him? Do not confuse wants with needs. Let us define *need as a physiological or psychological requirement for a person's life and well-being.* You *need* air in order to live. You have about a three-minute supply of oxygen that is being circulated around in your bloodstream right now. Three minutes without air and your brain cells will start dying. The eventual end of an unmet need is death or total dysfunction. *If you can live and function without it, it is not a need.* Think about all the different things you have ever wanted in life. The list could quickly grow to number into the thousands. Think about the things you have received. No matter how humble your situation is or has been in the past, chances are that quite a few of your wants have been met. Moreover, no matter how well to do you are now or have been in the past, chances are that you have not gotten everything you ever wanted. Either state puts you in a great place where you can understand this next statement. *There is a life and death difference between wants and needs.*

The sexiest, most fascinating, and frightening thing in the world to a man is a woman who does not need him—whether he just met her at the park or she's his girlfriend, fiancée, or wife of twenty-two years.

I think the keyword in the previous statement is the word "need." Remember, if a need goes unmet, then the person in need will die or become so dysfunctional that he or she might as well be dead. Neediness reeks of dependency, weakness, and vulnerability. Like predators, the easy kill will draw in most players and all dogs. However, the thought that a woman does not need them drives many mature men into the mode of, "I'll show you just how much you really need a man like me."

The Real Power of Being

The real power of being is the power to choose. I say that *the ultimate gift of life is the ability to choose.* I know that this may be another hard concept to grasp and accept, but I promise you that if you dare to accept this challenge, it will help to transform your life. The concept that you are empowered to change your life by changing your choices is not new at all, though it may be new to you. Your life situation is the sum total of all of the choices made by you and others. When we were children, the responsibility of those choices rested totally with the supervising adults in our lives. As we grow up, the responsibility of choice is shifted more onto us.

Most everything you do and do not do is a choice—from what time you get out of bed to what time you go to sleep at night. While we are on this subject of choice, I might as well go ahead and tell you that for the most part, your ignorance is also a choice. I cannot speak Japanese. My inability to speak Japanese is not because I am not Japanese; it is because I have chosen not to enroll in Japanese classes. I choose not to buy tapes or videos that could teach me as much of the Japanese language as I choose to learn. I chose not to be a doctor when I chose to be a teacher.

If you so choose, you can end most of the unhappiness in your life today and start living a life of joy. Being happy or unhappy is a choice based on your present conditions and circumstances. You have preset those circumstances and conditions that will make you happy. Happiness is very dependent on the preset events. What happens when your preset conditions for happiness are not met? That is right. You are not happy. Living in this manner puts you in the same position that most people find themselves in today: living a life in which every moment of happiness is entirely dependent on chance. I believe that life is far too short to live on chance. I believe that choice is a much better option. Now read what Robert J. Hastings had to say about happiness and choice: "*Places and circumstances never guarantee happiness. You must decide within yourself whether you want to be happy.*"

In addition to happiness, there is another choice called joy. Joy is a mind-set, an attitude, if you will. Real joy is much more than the denial of reality. *Denial is a lie you tell yourself to lessen the pain of not meeting the conditions you have set for happiness.* Denial is a choice to omit most of the negatives associated with life.

Joy is a choice to make the best out of the worst and learn as much as you can through the process. Joy is choosing to do more than cry about your lemons, but after you have counted all the lemons you have to deal with, you make lemonade.

Take your mess and make fertilizer out of it. Put it under your feet and grow, baby, grow! Maybe the choice of joy is too deep for you at this stage of your personal development or recovery; let us agree that your happiness is your personal responsibility. It is not his or anybody else's; it has to be yours. Either you set the criteria and parameters for your happiness or others will do it for you. If you can handle this, then the next step is to redefine or reselect your criteria for happiness. A word of caution to all: *This is not meant to be a key to the door to self-gratification. Remember that the new criterion is to enhance and improve your life, not devalue and destroy yourself.*

Being Alone Is Not Equal to Being Lonely

P erhaps one of the most misunderstood and under-appreciated states of life is the state of being alone. Being alone is a choice. I am not pushing for total isolation or total self-reliance, but I do want to add value and insight to the choice of being alone. There is no other time in a person's life that his or her mind is as free as when one is alone. The freedom to be yourself is at its all-time high when you are alone. The pressures to impress and influence others are gone. You may be surprised to see how good it is to spend a weekend alone. Leave the bestseller on the table. Turn off the TV. Eliminate all of the distractions we enjoy so much and get together with you. Talk to you to find out who you really are and what you really want to accomplish in your lifetime.

Being lonely is a choice. Being alone and being lonely are not synonymous, nor are they opposite sides of the same coin. Loneliness is an emotion—a feeling of isolation and separation without purpose. It is true that they are both choices you make, but being alone should have a purpose and a goal. I do not believe that being alone should ever be a by-product of personality or lifestyle. I know that if you are motivated to put into practice any of the choices I have set before you in this book, you may have to move away from your present peer group. However, you will be moving toward a new peer group at the same time who shares many of your new life goals. The great inventor Alexander Graham Bell put it like this, "When one door closes, another opens; but we often look so long and so regretfully upon the closed door that we do not see the one which has opened for us."

Stop Being So Stupid

One of the most unbelievable things I have encountered in my life is the sheer number of women who find themselves stuck in the revolving door of bad relationships. It is as though they believe it is their job in life to find and occupy the time and attention of every player, deadbeat loser, and dog that comes by, so that all the other women can safely get involved with the good men in meaningful relationships.

So, to all the minesweepers out there, I simply say, "Stop being so stupid." Before you throw this book down for the tenth-plus time, let me offer you this three-part definition of "stupid."

Part one—Stupid is when you know that an action is wrong or a situation is bad, but you still commit the act or get into the situation.

Part two—You know what the right thing to do is, but you do not do it.

Part three (The Catch All)—You have no reason whatsoever to do the action but you do it anyway.

Allow me to add that stupidity is—yes, you guessed it—a choice, not a condition. Stupidity is not a permanent state of being. As soon as you choose to stop participating in the stupidity, you stop being stupid. I am a black male. No matter what I decide to do or not to do, I am still a black male. A black male is not what I am being; it is simply a part of what I am. I used the word "part" because I want you to know that you are much more than your sex and peer group. Another thing we must remember is that conditions and situations we create while we are involved in our stupidity will, for the most part, last long beyond our participation in the stupidity.

The opposite of stupidity is being smart. Being smart is also a choice. Being smart is when you choose to utilize all of your knowledge and experience, as well as that of others, to your benefit and the benefit of others. Being smart and being intelligent have little to do with each other. Intelligence is beyond choice; it is your inborn ability to learn at a given rate. Because a person can learn information at a rapid rate does not ensure that the person will learn it and then utilize that information to benefit him or herself or others. The opposite of intelligence is dumb. Dumb is the total lack of intelligence, no innate ability to learn. The very fact that you are reading this book should be enough evidence to let you know that you are not dumb. Another definition I think will be of some use is that of the word ignorance. Ignorance is the lack of information; you simply do not know. Know that all of humankind suffers from ignorance, some of us much more than the rest of us.

For many women, there is a strong drive to have a functional, successful, long-term relationship with a man. This drive or desire can push them into a pattern of behaviors that is best described as insanity. My favorite definition of insanity is the one by Albert Einstein, "Doing the same thing over and over again and expecting different results." To put one's hand into a pot of hot water once may be an accident, but to put your hand into that same hot water expecting it to feel good the next time is insanity. Much of what we call *faithfulness* in a relationship is really *insanity*.

What Is This Thing We Call Love, Anyway?

I believe that the carrot that gets the cart moving in most of our relationships is the pursuit of love. If there is someone telling you that he loves you or is in love with you, ask him what he means when he says, "I love you." Ask the next ten people you meet what is love. Call your three best friends on the phone and ask them, "What is this thing we call love?" Note the wide range and varied responses you will receive. Little wonder there is so much confusion in and over the relationships that are supposed to be love based. Love is not an emotion. Love is far beyond the frailty of feelings in its stability and longevity. Love is nothing you can make. It is far too perfect to be the product of the imperfect. Love is not anything you fall into. It is too purposeful to be the result of an accident.

Love is the conscious decision to demonstrate at all times the highest character in all circumstances by putting the needs of another person in front of your needs—their wants in front of your wants. Then, you give your time, abilities, and assets to meet their needs to the point of death and their wants to the point of their satisfaction.

It is impossible to understand love without understanding each of the key words in the definition. By the end of this book, I will have exposed you to all of them. *Needs, others,* and *conscious decision* (choice) are at the heart of love. Note the order and what is *not* said in the definition. Needs must come first. Remember that a *need is necessary for life to continue. A want stems from a desire.* Satisfaction of desires may add to the perceived quality of life, but it is not necessary to sustain life.

Not all things are equal. Needs are equal to needs and wants are equal to wants. Never put another person's wants in front of your needs and call it love. That is stupid! If you needed to buy some lifesaving medicine and your loved one wanted some candy and you only had enough money to get one or the other, you would be stupid to buy the candy.

Another very important word found in the definition of love is the word *time.* Of all the great gifts and assets we have or could ever acquire, time is the most valuable. You can replace almost anything but time. Unlike money, once you spend it, it is gone forever. It may seem like a misspelling at first glance, but you could spell love another way—T-I-M-E—and be absolutely right.

To give your time is to give your love. Allow me to offer you the key to time: T is for Talent. I is for Involvement. M is for Money. E is for Emotions. All are essential elements to express love.

I want to add this little note to your insight. The opposite of love is not hate, as many people assume. When you understand real love, it is easy to see that the opposite of love is selfishness. Selfishness is that inborn desire to make sure that we take care of our needs and wants even at the expense of others.

What Do You Call a Friend?

I think that one of the major problems we have with relationships is that of misidentification or classification. We all have a group of relations we call "friends." Most of us have used this word far too loosely to have an understanding of its true depth.

Let us do an experiment: Count in your mind the number of friends you have. Note that any friend is a good friend. Take your time. Now write their names down on a piece of paper or a note pad. Stop. Now read this: *A friend is a person who wants what is best for you in every situation and in every circumstance and will help you to acquire the best for your own benefit. A friend will go through it (the circumstances and the situation) with you and for you, and the "it" does not matter.* Now rethink how many friends you really have. If you have four to five, you are an extraordinary person. If you have ten or more, you are dreaming. Wake up and reread the definition. I feel the need to tell some of you to avoid getting friends and family confused. Just because someone is family does not automatically make that person your friend. She may be your sister by birth, but she can only be your friend by choice.

It may seem that friendship is just another word for love. With friends, the focus is on the person, not the choice itself. Yet, I do admit it would be a job to comb out the difference between love and friendship.

All of Us Need C.A.R.E.

C.A.R.E. is my acronym for Celebration, Affection, Respect, and Encouragement. Perhaps the most important function of any relationship is the giving and receiving of C.A.R.E. I do not think that any one person can be the total source of anyone's C.A.R.E. Due to the importance of C.A.R.E., most of us rely on a network of people to supply the needed C.A.R.E.

Celebration of the *person* is the aim, not any personal accomplishments. We all need to have our person, the unique individual we are, celebrated. How well our person is celebrated has a great influence on our personal development. How does one celebrate the person of an individual? An oldie but goodie is the birthday celebration. The purpose of a birthday party is to celebrate the fact that you were born. The day became extra special because you were born on it. Another way to celebrate your person is to treat yourself to a favorite outing just for being you.

Affection is the open expression of intimacy. I like to say that intimacy is the need we all have to share our genuine person with others. Males often misidentify the need for affection as the need for sex. True affection and intimacy are tied together by the sincere desire to be known by others as we know ourselves and to know others as they know themselves. The expressions of intimacy (affection) can take many different forms like a simple note or *sharing* a personal poem or *sharing* your personal insights on a topic of special interest. True intimacy is not only *sharing* the best of times but the worst of times as well. The look of intimacy is that of oneness. If you have the pleasure of knowing a real close set of friends or a couple that has been close for a long time, often they start to look alike. I like to think that they have *shared* so much of what is on the inside of them with each other that it starts to show up on the outside. The only way to express intimacy is in the willful act of *sharing.* You cannot force people into intimacy; you can only earn the privilege over time. You need to know that it is possible to fake both intimacy and affection for a short time. The most likely reason for this type of deception is manipulation.

Respect is often quoted as the Golden Rule. "Do unto others as you would have others do unto you." This quote is interpreted as instruction to treat people the way you want to be treated in a given situation. Due to the great range of likes and personalities in your family—let alone between you and the rest of the world—I think that a more clear explanation is to treat people the way *they* want to be treated in a given situation. Respect of this manner is to pay respect to the person instead of the rule, which I think is the intent of the rule in the first place.

Encouragement is *to inspire with courage or confidence.* I think that the most meaningful form of encouragement is *help.* All of us need some help to reach a higher level of success. There is no such thing as pulling yourself up by your own bootstraps. Encouragement is much more than a cheerleader far removed from the action shouting cute memorized phrases for the benefit of spectators. We need coaches to help us with techniques and strategies to improve our chances and level of success. We need teammates who are living through the same experiences to give us a shoulder to lean on, a pat on the back, or a kick in the butt when needed.

You must also be willing and able to C.A.R.E. for yourself. No one can or should provide all of your C.A.R.E. for you. All others can do is to C.A.R.E. with you and in spite of you. No one else can C.A.R.E. for you any more than any one else can breathe for you. I am not saying you can or should be the only source of your C.A.R.E. However, you are the only source of your own personal C.A.R.E. You never want to ask others to do for you what you will not do for yourself and others. That would make you a user of people instead of one who utilizes her friends. Allowing yourself to receive C.A.R.E. from others is a form of self-C.A.R.E. as well. *Celebration, Affection, Respect,* and *Encouragement* can and should be a part of your personal self-treatment.

Rules of a Solid Relationship

I want to share with you eight rules that, if applied to all of your relationships, will help you to develop into the person you are seeking to be.

Rule #1: Never initiate a relationship with a male.

Whoever starts the relationship bears the major responsibility of maintaining it. I know that times have changed and that things are different, but they have not changed that much. You never want to be the one who has the most responsibility for the life and health of the relationship. That should be his job. If you take on that responsibility, you have set yourself up for some hard times for the life of the relationship. I know he is cute or so sweet and you are just dying to talk to him. You cannot wait any longer, so you call him first. You take the initiative and start the ball rolling in the relationship. After two weeks, the ball starts to slow down. You think a date would add a little pep. You are already trapped into fixing what you started. You are now calling him more than he is calling you. You are planning dates and outings. The list goes on and on, and the roles will never reverse. When you reverse from the traditional norms, the female is then subject to the same stresses and pressures her male counterpart has always had to endure as the initiator. The recipient of your attention is not in any way obligated to meet you half way. After you have had enough of this and are worn down by the lack of balance in the effort to grow and develop the relationship, you confront him about it. Do not be surprised when you hear these words from that sweet, quiet young man: "You called me first. I did not call you. Girl, you started this, not me. You are the one who hollered at me first."

Rule #2: You must first be in control, and then move to influence.

As a matter of life and death, you must first be in control of the relationship until you trust him enough to exchange control for influence. You must set the direction and speed at which the relationship moves. Influence is far better and more powerful than control, but control must come first. You must exchange influence for influence. When you are making the transition from control to influence, you must give into his influence only as much as he submits to your influence with him. Control has limitations that are so great that if the relationship never makes the transformation to influence, you will only have created a dictatorship instead of a relationship. The danger of this is simple to understand: you will now be in a so-called relationship with a man for whom you have little to no respect. No woman can respect any man she can control. The lack of respect will most often lead to some form of mistreatment or abuse. In order to be in control, you must be physically present with the person or thing you have control over. You have to be there in the same physical location, or at least able to talk to the one who is under your control. There are a great number of abused males out there. Know that the male victim of abuse is more likely to respond with physical violence than his female counterpart. This does not mean that you are the one who abused him, nor is it a way to excuse him of any acts of violence toward you or anybody else. I simply want to let you know that in most cases the male you are or will be involved with is damaged goods. You must remember that your life is in danger. In the United States, most women who are killed are killed by a man who has sworn to love her "until death do us part" or a boyfriend or some male who has told her, "I love you." I know this is a grim way to approach any relationship, but we are talking about real-life situations. Look at headlines in any newspaper. If there is a female victim, repeatedly the number one suspect and later convicted perpetrator is the husband, ex-husband, boyfriend, ex-boyfriend, lover, or ex-lover.

Rule #3: Demand nothing less than everything he has.

The best option I have ever heard of for going the right way and ending up the right way is to start the right way. If you settle for less at the start of a relationship, you have just settled for less for the entire relationship. Whenever I talk about everything he has, I am not talking about a prenuptial agreement. Remember that possessions are never the prize in any relationship—the person is. To think otherwise is to prostitute yourself to the highest bidder. You are not after his possessions. This "everything" I refer to is him. His best effort to ensure your presence in his life and his heart is the "everything" I am talking about. If you get his heart, you get all of him and all of his possessions.

A man's heart is his everything. It must be everything you are for everything he is. Make it an even trade or do not trade at all. Never trade your heart for his possessions. If you do, you will always get the short end of the stick. Do not worry, though. If you are the one for him, it is his job to convince you that he is the one for you. The world has countless women who have settled for a man's stuff. They married the stuff and later found themselves alone with none, some, or all of the stuff but not him. Men can buy and make more stuff. Men have only one heart to give. Remember rule number one. Do not break it, and you are in the driver's seat.

Rule #4: Never over-invest in the relationship.

Few people would argue when I say that by far, most women invest more of themselves and do so far sooner than the men in the average relationship. To over-invest is to put more of you into the relationship than he does. This creates an imbalance in power that is not in your favor. You become top heavy and can easily fall headlong into a dangerous relationship. Always care less than he does. The one who cares the least has the most power and control. Remember: when the time is right, you will exchange control for influence. The right time is after he has won your deepest trust, and not one second sooner.

Rule 5: Evaluate the relationship.

In order to track and gauge the condition of anything, it

has to be evaluated. I recommend weekly evaluations for all of your relationships. To assist in this task, I offer you the two-H system: Help and Hinder. You evaluate the relationship based on which "H" you are receiving more of from the relationship. You may find that many of your girlfriend relationships will not survive or score highly in light of this evaluation. Every significant relationship you have is either helping you reach your goals or hindering you from reaching your goals. You must decide if each relationship is worth your valuable time or not. If you find that the relationship is a hindrance, end it. The sooner you end a hindering relationship, the better you are positioned for success in life.

Rule 6: Always go with performance.

There are three P's that can draw a woman to a man's side. They are promise, potential, and performance. A promise is what he says he is going to do. Ask yourself just how many times in your life you have said or heard, "But you promised me ..." You must learn to guard your heart against his promises. Promises sound good. They always do. How's this for a promise: "I promise you that I will do all I can to make you trust in me and believe all I say to you so that I can have sex with you as soon as I can and as often as I want until I am tired of you. Then, I will leave you for the next girl who catches my attention." You will never hear this kind of promise. You may have lived it, but you will never hear it.

The next "P" is potential. Many women are drawn to a man's potential and talent. They dream of what could be if her man could only get a break. Potential is common to us all, but for some reason some seem to have far more of it than others do. A newspaper reporter once said to Vince Dooley, former head football coach and athletic director of the University of Georgia, that his UGA Bulldog football team "had a lot of potential this year." Coach Dooley replied, "Potential means you haven't done a darn thing yet." Life is far too short to waste precious time on what could be.

The third "P" is performance. Performance is the key to guarding your heart against promises and potential. It is not what you say you will do. It is not what you have the ability to do. It is simply what you do that makes the difference. Ben Franklin once said, "*Well done is better than well said.*" It may help you to understand the way most men understand life. Most men deal with the bottom line. The bottom line is that promises and potential do not mean a thing. The only thing that counts is performance. He promised to make the basket. He has the potential to make the shot. All of this sounds good, but the score changes only if the ball goes through the hoop.

Rule 7: All important relationships are expensive.

The only question is how much of you and yours you are willing to give in time and other assets to help grow and maintain the relationship. *Never* give up anything that you cannot live without for any relationship. Therefore, the obvious question is, "How much should I be willing to give to help grow and develop this relationship?" It makes no sense at all to die for a relationship that you do not need to live. Your virginity, family, self-respect, health, and life are far too valuable to give for any relationship.

Rule 8: Do not give him too much ammunition too soon.

What I mean by this is do not give him too much information about you too soon. Let him expose himself to you more than you do to him. You had better get this. A player will use every bit of information you give him against you to get what he really wants. Every expressed weakness, every hope, dream, and desire is the ammunition he will use to wage war against your defenses to wear them down and take advantage of you. Do not confuse treasure with information. You are the treasure he is to seek. To the player, information is just the kind of ammunition he is looking for to use on you.

How Do You Tell the One Who Stays from the One Who Plays?

Please let me get right to the point here. Shut up and listen. You talk too much. He is not your girlfriend. The number one goal of the player is to get you talking to him. He knows that if he can get you to do this, it is just a matter of time before he has you right where he wants you. The old saying goes, "Talk is cheap," but in this case, talking can cost you your life. The more you share your needs, wants, feelings, dreams, and hopes, the easier it is to predict and induce your thinking.

It is all about your heart and mind. Know that the heart and the mind are the same. If he ever figures out how your mind works and how to get you to think the way he wants you to think about him, yourself, and life in general, it is all over. Now you belong to him. If he gets you to this point, he is now the master, and you are the slave. This is the same path that pimp uses to lead a prostitute to his corner. What do you think happened to get her out on that corner in any weather for her man? The pimp simply found the way to reach her mind. He listened to her talk about her dreams and her story of pain. He learned about her fears and her ambitions. Then he manipulated her words to trap her with his lies. Through his words, he captured her heart. When anybody has your heart, they have you and all that comes with you.

Turn the tables by closing your mouth and opening your eyes and ears. Know that the first goal of communication is to understand. The second goal of communication is then to be understood. Get to know him better and before he gets to know you.

To tell who and what you are dealing with, you must learn to look and listen. Hear what he is saying to you and what he is not saying. Listen. Does he talk of having a family, owning a business, or going back to school? If you listen long enough, hard enough, and understand deep enough, you will be able to tell who and what you are dealing with. Having heard him, you now have all the information you need to compare what he says to what he does. If you find a big difference between the two, be afraid—be very afraid. Remember the three P's. Performance should rule the day.

Sticks and snakes look the same in the dark or low light. In order to truly know the male with whom you are dealing, he must be seen in the bright light of knowledge. Ignorance is darkness. Knowledge is light. Until you know the truth about him, you are in the dark. The real person is the one behind the eyes and the smile. He is deeper than his skin and his jeans.

While we are talking about the mind and listening, I want to give you a great little evaluation tool to help you determine the level of the mind you have and the one with which you are dealing. This tool can also be a great aid in your own personal mental development as well.

The next few words can help improve your assessment of the attitude of every person you talk or listen to. Simply put, great minds think and talk about ideals, average minds think and talk about events, and small minds think and talk about people.

The Real Person Is Found in the Character, Not the Personality

Personality is the conscious self-image we choose to display in public. It is the outward show we put on for our adoring public. It is the image we desire for others to see. Personality is our shallow, surface self. All of us can play the chameleon when it comes to personality. The true, deeper self is called character. To get to know the real person, you must get past personality to the character. Character is the subconscious self that is revealed as one reacts to life's most stressful situations and circumstances. Character is revealed when we face the heat and pressures of life.

The tea is in the bag, not the box. What I mean by this is that he may come in a tall, dark, and handsome box, but when you put the contents in some hot water for a while, you may find that the box is misleading. Remember always: choose contents over the container. A well-known speaker and lecturer on leadership named John Maxwell said, "Circumstances do not make you what you are—they reveal what you are!" I want you to know that noble character is one of your greatest possessions. If you lose all your material things, all of your physical abilities, all of your personal relationships, but still have a noble character, you are a winner. Character will determine the level of real success you will have in forming valuable and lasting personal relationships.

The Real Test of a Relationship

The real decisive tests of any relationship are conflict and adversity. The relationship must pass the fire test, as well as the time test. Like fire, conflict and adversity will either consume or refine a relationship. If the relationship cannot survive conflict and adversity, then it does not need or deserve to survive.

Conflict and adversity are both very important parts of life that cannot be avoided for any long stretch of time. If you are looking for a relationship that will be void of conflict and involve two people who are both alive, stop wasting your time. All of us have internal conflicts with ourselves. We think one way but behave in another. We want to be a certain type of person that we are not. We smile when we feel like crying. How can we ever hope to have a relationship with another internally conflicted person and it be free of conflicts?

The key is for you to master and teach positive, productive ways to manage conflict, not waste precious time trying to place blame on someone else, or eliminate, avoid, or deny that the conflict exists. The better the conflict management, the better the relationship that can develop.

I do not recommend picking fights in any relationship, neither do I recommend running from them. However, I will say this: never commit to a relationship with anybody if you have not seen how he or she deals with conflict and adversity. You need to know up front if he is a hitter, a quitter, a pouter, or a shouter. You need to know if he can sit down and talk to you like a man or if he runs home and tells his mother and his boys everything.

His Toys May Be a Trap Set for You

Do not fall for his toys and trappings. Money, cars, clothes, cell phones, iPods, or the latest hot ticket item can easily sidetrack your mind and keep your attention away from the real issue, which is the kind of person you are dealing with. Just like the "real" you is the treasure, so is the "real" him. Do not allow yourself to be shallow and materialistic. When it is all said and done, you must remember that the real man makes the stuff, and the stuff can never make a real man. Some men may offer you expensive gifts early in the relationship. You would be wise to say no. This may be a test to see if you really want him or his stuff. Know that if you ever sell out once for the stuff, in his mind you are paid in full for life. You become the latest addition to his bought property, like his truck, bike, or bowling ball. You are now simply a part of his collection of things, and he will manage you, but most likely he will never be in love with you.

Separate the Men from the Boys

What kryptonite is to Superman, a silver bullet is to a werewolf, and the sun is to a vampire, commitment is to the player. The very mention of a long-term, monogamous commitment sends shivers down the spine of any real player.

What distinguishes the men from the boys is the man's ability to make, keep, and grow a commitment to a personal relationship and the responsibilities that come along with it. Real men have developed in themselves the personal fortitude to keep on keeping on in a relationship in spite of challenging situations and circumstances. Real men can commit to the commitment. I know that you want him committed to you alone. You somehow got it into your head that you are worth it—and you are. However, because you are a work in progress—always changing—if his commitment is to you alone, then it is to you as you are. What happens when you change? That is right. Then the object of his commitment has changed. If he based his commitment on you alone, then he has no recourse but to change or abandon his commitment to you. Your best course of action is to first be honest with yourself about who you really are and recognize that you are growing and changing as you develop new skills and abilities. At this point, you must be willing to apply the Rules of a Solid Relationship, understanding that the relationship might not survive.

I think you need to know with whom you are dealing from the start. Up front—from the start of the relationship—while you are in the control phase, let him know that only serious applicants need apply. If your candor frightens or intimidates him, he is not the one. Any male who is intimidated by your realness is not man enough for you. He must respect you but never be intimidated by you. You can never have a close, lasting relationship with anyone who is or who can be intimidated by you. People who are intimidated by you will find a way to hurt you. It is not a matter of if they will hurt you, but when and how. This is true for all would-be friends, females as well as males.

Dating and Courtship Are Bad Choices of Terms and Even Worse Activities

When you understand the origin of the terms dating and courtship, it puts them in a different light. Do a little research and you will see what I am about to say to you is true. It is just as true now as it was three thousand years ago. In the homes and palaces of the kings and the very rich of the Far East, the king, or master, of the home kept a group of young women available to him and his favorite acquaintances for their sexual satisfaction. This group of women was called a harem. They were kept in separate chambers, or living quarters, from the wives, the family, and the rest of the household. Sometimes the members of the harem were bought outright as slaves. Often the members were recruited throughout the kingdom. The families of the girls were often compensated by the king with land, government positions, and other favors for the use of their daughters and even sons in the harem. To ensure that the king had his choice of any in his harem for any given day or night, the young women were free to parade around in a highly exclusive and heavily guarded courtyard. There the king would go *courting* to find his delight for the night. One of the worst things that could happen would be if the king was attracted to someone in the courtyard and her menstrual cycle prevented her from being available to him. To safeguard against this tragedy, the court staff would painstakingly chart, or *date*, the menstrual cycle of each female court member. Once properly *dated*, the staff would know who to include or exclude based on her availability. Needless to say, *dating* was not necessary for the males of the court. The *dating* was also used to keep track of the king's offspring. Whoever the king "favored" became his exclusive property for as long as he desired. After he was finished with her, she became open game to his friends or even totally banned from the courtyard. In many instances, all favors done for the families were undone.

In life, you will find that relationships, romance, and reality seldom come as a neat, packaged deal. The three are like oil and vinegar in a bottle. The bottle is the relationship that has the capacity and strength to contain both liquids. The oil is symbolic of romance—light and full of spice and flavor. The vinegar is symbolic of reality—heavier than the oil—and it brings its own flavor, a balance of bitterness and sweetness to the mix. Within the confines of the relationship, the two may be in the same approximate space at the same time, but not together. To get them together, you must be willing to shake things up a bit. The more you shake, the better the mix.

Now if you are asking yourself the question, "If I don't date, then what do I do?" Where do you go from here? These questions remind me of the closing lines in the first *Matrix* movie. In this book, I have offered you a choice, only a choice, a chance at another life, another existence. You may end up alone but not lonely, unpopular but more powerful, less visited but more of a victor.

I am one of the ones who played the game and beat the odds. I came out of it alive, without an incurable disease, no babies outside of marriage. I suffered no jail time or even a criminal record. However, there was a price to pay; at this point, there is nothing I can do to get back the years and money I wasted being a player. I cannot make up for the time I wasted in the first ten years of my marriage unlearning the player's mind-set.

I offer this advice. Start with a worthwhile goal, a goal worthy of your time and effort, a project that is grand enough that when you accomplish it, it is worth you and your loved ones celebrating. Remember that the true greatness is measured in terms of how much you help others, not just yourself. Once you have a goal in mind, develop a plan to accomplish your goal. Make sure that the plan allows you to enjoy small and immediate success. For example, if your goal is to go to college to become a teacher in order to help children, develop your plan and make sure that you build in celebration checkpoints along the way. Step one: complete the college application and other needed papers, and get them in the mail. (Celebrate!) Step two: get accepted. (Celebrate!) Step three: get to the campus, register for class, and get books and a room. (Celebrate!) Get through the first grading period. (Celebrate!)

Allow me to caution you about the extent of your celebration. Do not be like the young man who wanted to save ten thousand dollars for a nice secondhand car, and to encourage himself he threw a party every time he saved a thousand dollars. The only problem was that each of his parties cost him a thousand dollars.

Last Thoughts from My Heart

This is the heart of a father to his children. My hope is to help, not hurt you. I know that much of what I said to you may be new, but all I ask is that you just look around and see if what I have tried to tell you is the truth. Go to some older man whom you trust—your father, perhaps a former player and now a father, an uncle, or a friend—and tell him what I said. Read to him the lines that give you the biggest problems and ask his opinion on them. Also, ask women whom you know to be strong and successful leaders for their insight on any of these topics. Nevertheless, having done all of this, it still comes down to the fact that you have to choose how you are going to live your life. As a reformed player, I have chosen to hate the game, not the players. I choose to hate the lies, the pain, and the suffering that come with the whole game. If it were up to me, the whole game would be done away with right now and forever. Few, if any, of us can truly say that we have lived our lives and have not been hurt in some way by the games that players play.

As I have told you, I was schooled in the rules of

the game from boyhood, but what I did not tell you was that throughout the entire time my father was completely silent to me about my relationships with girls. He never once told me to save myself for my wife. I know that I have told you that it is up to you to make your own choices. I want to give a word of encouragement to the fathers out there: please talk to your daughters and sons. Share your heart with them about your hopes for them. You may not agree with everything I shared in this book, so share with them what you do believe. My father was not one of my teachers in the art of the game, but he could have ended the game for me with just a few of the words I have shared with you. Had he told me the importance of keeping myself until marriage or the dangers of being a player, it would have given me a choice. I just hope that some of what I said gives you a choice.

This book is my response to my dislike for the game and my love for the many young women it has been my blessing to know, love, and protect. I have chosen to look at the player with empathy, not hatred, because I have been there and done that, and I have the scars to prove it.

To all the people I have hurt along the way as I played the game, all I can offer now are my apologies. I hope that you, too, have found that real life is game free.

Glossary of Terms

Attitude—Your chosen basic outlook on life. It is the way you decide to see people, events, and the stages of life.

Abstinence—Not engaging in physical contact of any kind that has the intended purpose of giving or receiving pleasure of a sexual nature.

C.A.R.E.—Celebration, Affection, Respect, Encouragement.

Character—The subconscious self that is revealed as one reacts to life's situations and circumstances.

Contentment—A mind-set or attitude that is the result of a personal recognition and uncomplaining acceptance of the truth that the life they are living is far better than they deserve.

Discipline—The mental ability to say no to a choice now in order to say yes to a better choice later or the same choice at a better time, or saying yes to a choice that at the present is unpleasant or downright painful in order to enjoy a higher level of success and enjoyment later.

Dumb—A total lack of intelligence; the innate inability to learn.

Friend—A person who wants what's best for you in every situation and in every circumstance and will help you to acquire the best for your own benefit. A friend will go through it with you and for you, and the "it" (the circumstances and the situation) does not matter.

Happiness—An emotional state based on your present conditions and circumstances. You have pre-selected those conditions that will make you happy.

Herdsman—The type of player that seeks to keep a flock of females at his ready. He is after timid, docile, tamed, and settled females with a low self-esteem.

Hunter—The type of player that is after the trophy girl, the wild, independent, free-roaming female with a projected high self-esteem. The hunter enjoys the hunt. It is the thrill of the chase that he hungers for.

Hunter-Gatherer—The type of player that has the widest range of the players when it comes to the type of female he is after. The hunter-gatherer has the run of the field. He is just as comfortable with the timid sheep as he is giving chase to the wild doe.

Ignorance—A lack of information; you simply don't know.

Insanity—Repeating the same behavior over and over again expecting a different result.

Intelligence—An inborn ability to learn at a given rate.

Joy—A choice to make the best out of the worst and learn as much as you can through the process.

Loneliness—An emotion, a feeling of isolation and separation without purpose.

Love—A conscious decision to demonstrate at all times the highest character in all circumstances by putting the needs of another person in front of your needs and wants, then to give your time, abilities, and assets to meeting that person's needs to the point of death and his or her wants to the point of satisfaction.

Need—A physiological or psychological requirement for a person's survival and well-being.

Problem—Any situation or condition that causes you distress, difficulty, or trouble; it is your right and/or responsibility to find a solution.

Personality—The conscious self-image we choose to display in public. The outward show we put on for our adoring public. It is the image we desire others to see. Personality is our shallow, surface self.

Smart—Choosing to utilize all of your knowledge and experience, as well as that of others, to your benefit and the benefit of others.

Success—The product of accurate knowledge and timely disciplined application of that knowledge; it is not the by-product of luck and hard work.

Stupidity—1. Knowing that an action is wrong, but still doing it. A situation is bad, but you still get into it or stay in it. 2. Knowing the right thing to do, but not doing it. 3. Having no reason whatsoever to do something, but doing it anyway.

T.I.M.E.—Talent, Involvement, Money, Emotions.

Want—A feeling that stems from desire. It is not needed for survival.

Contact

Robert Williams is available for seminars, motivational speeches, lectures, and book signings.

Contact info:
robert@realwordonline.com
(706) 247-0278.

Purchase info:
http://www.tatepublishing.com/bookstore/
book.php?w=978-1-60604-148-2

Web address: www.realwordonline.com

Also, log on to realwordonline.com for information on Robert Williams' upcoming release, *Don't Tell Them I Can Read*, coming Summer 2009!